Network Analysis and Visualization in R

Alboukadel KASSAMBARA

ii

Published by STHDA (http://www.sthda.com), Alboukadel Kassambara

Contact: Alboukadel Kassambara <alboukadel.kassambara@gmail.com>

For general information contact Alboukadel Kassambara <alboukadel.kassambara@gmail.com>.

Contents

0.1 What you will learn iv
0.2 Book website iv
0.3 Colophon iv

About the author   **v**

1 Network Visualization Essentials   **1**
1.1 Introduction 1
1.2 Graph theory: Basics and key terms 1
1.3 Install required packages 2
1.4 Data structure 2
1.5 Tools and visualization 5
1.6 Graph layout 7
1.7 Read more 14

2 Network Analysis and Manipulation   **15**
2.1 Load required packages 15
2.2 Create network objects 15
2.3 Print out a network object 18
2.4 Network graph manipulation 19
2.5 Network analysis 21
2.6 Read more 24

3 Interactive Network Visualization   **25**
3.1 Load demo data sets and R package 25
3.2 networkD3 R package 25
3.3 visNetwork R package 29

Preface

0.1 What you will learn

Social network analysis is used to investigate the inter-relationship between entities. Examples of network structures, include: social media networks, friendship networks and collaboration networks.

This book provides a quick start guide to network analysis and visualization in R.

You'll learn, how to:

- Create static and interactive network graphs using modern R packages.
- Change the layout of network graphs.
- Detect important or central entities in a network graph.
- Detect community (or cluster) in a network.

0.2 Book website

http://www.sthda.com/english

0.3 Colophon

This book was built with R 3.3.2 and the following packages :

```
##           name version  source
## 1      ggraph   1.0.0    CRAN
## 2      igraph   1.1.2    cran
## 3   networkD3    0.4    CRAN
## 4   tidygraph   1.0.0    CRAN
## 5   tidyverse   1.1.1    CRAN
## 6  visNetwork   2.0.1    CRAN
```

About the author

Alboukadel Kassambara is a PhD in Bioinformatics and Cancer Biology. He works since many years on genomic data analysis and visualization (read more: `http://www.alboukadel.com/`).

He has work experiences in statistical and computational methods to identify prognostic and predictive biomarker signatures through integrative analysis of large-scale genomic and clinical data sets.

He created a bioinformatics web-tool named GenomicScape (www.genomicscape.com) which is an easy-to-use web tool for gene expression data analysis and visualization.

He developed also a training website on data science, named STHDA (Statistical Tools for High-throughput Data Analysis, www.sthda.com/english), which contains many tutorials on data analysis and visualization using R software and packages.

He is the author of many popular R packages for:

- multivariate data analysis (**factoextra**, `http://www.sthda.com/english/rpkgs/factoextra`),
- survival analysis (**survminer**, `http://www.sthda.com/english/rpkgs/survminer/`),
- correlation analysis (**ggcorrplot**, `http://www.sthda.com/english/wiki/ggcorrplot-visualization-of-a-correlation-matrix-using-ggplot2`),
- creating publication ready plots in R (**ggpubr**, `http://www.sthda.com/english/rpkgs/ggpubr`).

Recently, he published several books on data analysis and visualization:

1. Practical Guide to Cluster Analysis in R (`https://goo.gl/yhhpXh`)
2. Practical Guide To Principal Component Methods in R (`https://goo.gl/d4Doz9`)
3. R Graphics Essentials for Great Data Visualization (`https://goo.gl/oT8Ra6`)

ABOUT THE AUTHOR

Chapter 1

Network Visualization Essentials

1.1 Introduction

Network Analysis is used to investigate and visualize the inter-relationship between entities (individuals, things).

Examples of network structures, include: social media networks, friendship networks, collaboration networks and disease transmission.

Network and graph theory are extensively used across different fields, such as in biology (pathway analysis and protein-protein interaction visualization), finance, social sciences, economics, communication, history, computer science, etc.

In this chapter, you'll learn:

- the basic terms of network analysis and visualization.
- how to create static networks using igraph (R base plot) and ggraph (ggplot2 system) packages.

1.2 Graph theory: Basics and key terms

Network graphs are characterized by two key terms: **nodes** and **edges**

- **nodes**: The entities (individual actors, people, or things) to be connected in the network. Synonyms: **vertices** of a graph.

- **edges**: The connections (interactions or relationships) between the entities. Synonyms: **links**, **ties**.

- **adjacency matrix**: a square matrix in which the column and row names are the nodes of the network. This is a standard data format accepted by many network analysis packages in R. Synonyms: **sociomatrices**. Within the matrix a 1 specifies that there is a link between the nodes, and a 0 indicates no link.

- **edge list**: a data frame containing at least two columns: one column of nodes corresponding to the source of a connection and another column of nodes that contains the target of the connection. The nodes in the data are identified by unique IDs.

- **Node list**: a data frame with a single column listing the node IDs found in the edge list. You can also add attribute columns to the data frame such as the names of the nodes or grouping variables.

- **Weighted network graph**: An edge list can also contain additional columns describing **attributes** of the edges such as a magnitude aspect for an edge. If the edges have a magnitude attribute the graph is considered weighted.

- **Directed and undirected network graph**:

(i) If the distinction between source and target is meaningful, the **network is directed**. Directed edges represent an ordering of nodes, like a relationship extending from one nodes to another, where switching the direction would change the structure of the network. The World Wide Web is an example of a directed network because hyperlinks connect one Web page to another, but not necessarily the other way around (Tyner et al., 2017).

(ii) If the distinction is not meaningful, the **network is undirected**. Undirected edges are simply links between nodes where order does not matter. Co-authorship networks represent examples of undirected networks, where nodes are authors and they are connected by an edge if they have written a publication together (Tyner et al., 2017).

Another example: When people send e-mail to each other, the distinction between the sender (source) and the recipient (target) is clearly meaningful, therefore the network is directed.

1.3   Install required packages

- `navdata`: contains data sets required for this book
- `tidyverse`: for general data manipulation
- `igraph`, `tidygraph` and `ggraph`: for network visualization

1. Install the `navdata` R package:

```
if(!require(devtools)) install.packages("devtools")
devtools::install_github("kassambara/navdata")
```

2. Install the remaining packages:

```
install.packages(
  c("tidyverse", "igraph", "tidygraph", "ggraph")
)
```

1.4   Data structure

1.4.1 Demo data set

We'll use a fake demo data set containing the number of phone calls between the president of some EU countries.

```
library("navdata")
data("phone.call")
head(phone.call, 3)
```

```
##      source destination n.call
## 1   France     Germany      9
## 2  Belgium      France      4
## 3   France       Spain      3
```

> Nodes are countries in the source and destination columns. The values, in the column `n.call`, will be used as edges weight.

To visualize the network graph, we need to create two data frames from the demo data sets:

- **nodes list**: containing nodes labels and other nodes attributes
- **edges list**: containing the relationship between the nodes. It consists of the edge list and any additional edge attributes.

In the following sections, we start by creating nodes and edges lists. Next, we'll use the different packages to create network graphs.

1.4.2 Create nodes list

First, load the `tidyverse` R package for data manipulation:

```
library(tidyverse)
```

Then, compute the following key steps to create nodes list:

1. Take the distinct countries from both the "source" and "destination" columns
2. Change the column name to `label`
3. Join the information from the two columns together.

```
# Get distinct source names
sources <- phone.call %>%
  distinct(source) %>%
  rename(label = source)

# Get distinct destination names
destinations <- phone.call %>%
  distinct(destination) %>%
  rename(label = destination)

# Join the two data to create node
# Add unique ID for each country
```

```
nodes <- full_join(sources, destinations, by = "label")
nodes <- nodes %>%
  mutate(id = 1:nrow(nodes)) %>%
  select(id, everything())

head(nodes, 3)

## # A tibble: 3 x 2
##       id   label
##    <int>   <chr>
## 1     1   France
## 2     2  Belgium
## 3     3  Germany
```

1.4.3   Create edges list

Key steps:

1. Take the phone.call data, which are already in edges list format, showing the connection between nodes. Rename the column "n.call" to "weight".
2. Join the node IDs to the edges list data
   a. Do this for the "source" column and rename the id column that are brought over from nodes. New name: "from".
   b. Do this for the "destination" column and rename the id column. New name: "to"
   c. Select only the columns "from" and "to" in the edge data. We don't need to keep the column "source" and "destination" containing the names of countries. These information are already present in the node data.

```
# Rename the n.call column to weight
phone.call <- phone.call %>%
  rename(weight = n.call)


# (a) Join nodes id for source column
edges <- phone.call %>%
  left_join(nodes, by = c("source" = "label")) %>%
  rename(from = id)


# (b) Join nodes id for destination column
edges <- edges %>%
  left_join(nodes, by = c("destination" = "label")) %>%
  rename(to = id)


# (c) Select/keep only the columns from and to
edges <- select(edges, from, to, weight)
head(edges, 3)


## # A tibble: 3 x 3
```

```
##    from    to weight
##   <int> <int>  <dbl>
## 1     1     3      9
## 2     2     1      4
## 3     1     8      3
```

1.5 Tools and visualization

There are many tools and software to analyse and visualize network graphs. However, for a reproducible and automatized research you need a programming environment such as in R software.

In this section, we review major R packages for reproducible network analysis and visualization.

We'll introduce how to create static network graphs using `igraph` (file., 2017) and `tidygraph`(Pedersen, 2017b) + `ggraph` (Pedersen, 2017a) packages.

Note that, `igraph` packages uses the R base plotting system. The `ggraph` package is based on ggplot2 plotting system, which is highly flexible.

If you are new to network analysis in R, we highly recommend to learn the `tidygraph` and the `ggraph` package for the analysis and the visualization, respectively.

> Note that, each time that you create a network graph, you need to set the random generator to always have the same layout. For example, you can type type this: `set.seed(123)`

1.5.1 igraph

1. **Create an igraph network object**:

- Key R function: `graph_from_data_frame()`.

- Key arguments:

    - `d`: edge list
    - `vertices`: node list
    - `directed`: can be either TRUE or FALSE depending on whether the data is directed or undirected.

```
library(igraph)
net.igraph <- graph_from_data_frame(
  d = edges, vertices = nodes,
  directed = TRUE
  )
```

2. **Create a network graph with igraph**

```
set.seed(123)
plot(net.igraph, edge.arrow.size = 0.2,
     layout = layout_with_graphopt)
```

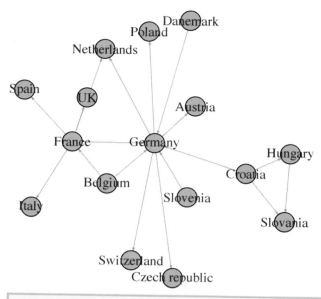

> See the documentation by typing `?plot.igraph`, for more options to customize the plot.

1.5.2   tidygraph and ggraph

`tidygraph` and `ggraph` are modern R packages for network data manipulation (`tidygraph`) and visualization (`ggraph`). They leverage the power of igraph.

1. **Create a network object using tidygraph:**

- Key function: `tbl_graph()`.
- key arguments: `nodes`, `edges` and `directed`.

```
library(tidygraph)
net.tidy <- tbl_graph(
  nodes = nodes, edges = edges, directed = TRUE
  )
```

2. **Visualize network using ggraph**

Key functions:

- `geom_node_point()`: Draws node points.

- `geom_edge_link()`: Draws edge links. To control the width of edge line according to the weight variable, specify the option `aes(width = weight)`, where, the weight specify the number of phone.call sent along each route. In this case, you can control the maximum and minimum width of the edges, by using the function scale_edge_width() to set the range (minimum and maximum width value). For example: scale_edge_width(range = c(0.2, 2)).

- geom_node_text(): Adds text labels for nodes, by specifying the argument aes(label = label). To avoid text overlapping, indicate the option repel = TRUE.

- labs(): Change main titles, axis labels and legend titles.

Create a classic node-edge diagrams. Possible values for the argument layout include: 'star', 'circle', 'gem', 'dh', 'graphopt', 'grid', 'mds', 'randomly', 'fr', 'kk', 'drl', 'lgl'.

```
library(ggraph)
ggraph(net.tidy, layout = "graphopt") +
  geom_node_point() +
  geom_edge_link(aes(width = weight), alpha = 0.8) +
  scale_edge_width(range = c(0.2, 2)) +
  geom_node_text(aes(label = label), repel = TRUE) +
  labs(edge_width = "phone.call") +
  theme_graph()
```

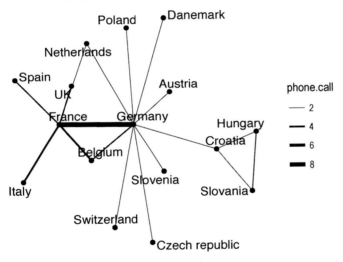

1.6 Graph layout

Layout defines the placement of nodes and edges in a given graph structure. There are different types of possible layouts (https://www.data-imaginist.com/2017/ggraph-introduction-layouts/). You should use the layout that suit the best your graph data structure.

In this section, we'll describe some of the layouts, including:

- linear: Arranges the nodes linearly or circularly in order to make an arc diagram.

- `treemap`: Creates a treemap from the graph, that is, a space-filing subdivision of rectangles showing a weighted hierarchy.

1.6.1 Arc diagram layout

In the following example, we'll:

- Layout the nodes linearly (horizontal line) using `layout = "linear"`.
- Create an arc diagram by drawing the edges as arcs
- Add only the label names, instead of including node points.

> In the following arc diagram, the edges above the horizontal line move from left to right, while the edges below the line move from right to left.

```
# Arc diagram
ggraph(net.tidy, layout = "linear") +
  geom_edge_arc(aes(width = weight), alpha = 0.8) +
  scale_edge_width(range = c(0.2, 2)) +
  geom_node_text(aes(label = label), repel = TRUE) +
  labs(edge_width = "Number of calls") +
  theme_graph()+
  theme(legend.position = "top")
```

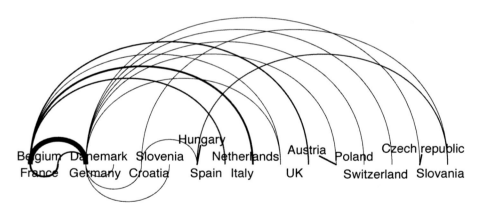

```
# Coord diagram, circular
ggraph(net.tidy, layout = "linear", circular = TRUE) +
  geom_edge_arc(aes(width = weight), alpha = 0.8) +
  scale_edge_width(range = c(0.2, 2)) +
  geom_node_text(aes(label = label), repel = TRUE) +
  labs(edge_width = "Number of calls") +
  theme_graph()+
  theme(legend.position = "top")
```

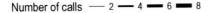

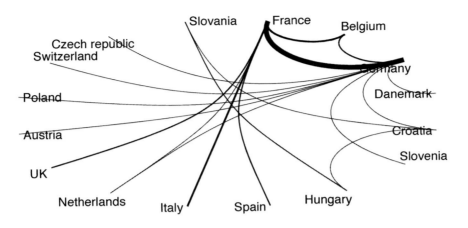

1.6.2 Treemap layout

A treemap is a visual method for displaying hierarchical data that uses nested rectangles to represent the branches of a tree diagram. Each rectangles has an area proportional to the amount of data it represents.

To illustrate this layout, we'll use the `france.trade` demo data set [in `navdata` package].
It contains the trading percentage between France and different countries.

1.6.2.1 Demo data sets

```
data("france.trade")
france.trade

## # A tibble: 251 x 3
##    source destination trade.percentage
##     <chr>       <chr>            <dbl>
## 1 France        Aruba            0.035
## 2 France Afghanistan             0.035
## 3 France       Angola            0.035
## 4 France     Anguilla            0.035
## 5 France      Albania            0.035
## 6 France      Finland            0.035
## # ... with 245 more rows
```

1.6.2.2 Nodes list

Nodes are the distinct countries in the source and the destination columns.

1. Take the distinct countries and create the nodes list:

```
# Distinct countries
countries <- c(
  france.trade$source, france.trade$destination
) %>%
  unique()
# Create nodes list
nodes <- data_frame(
  id = 1:length(countries),
  label = countries
)
```

2. Bind the trade percentage and turn the NAs into 0:

```
nodes <- nodes %>%
  left_join(
    france.trade[, c("destination", "trade.percentage")],
    by = c("label" = "destination" )
    ) %>%
  mutate(
    trade.percentage = ifelse(
      is.na(trade.percentage), 0, trade.percentage
      )
  )
head(nodes, 3)

## # A tibble: 3 x 3
##      id       label trade.percentage
##    <int>      <chr>            <dbl>
## 1    1      France            0.000
## 2    2       Aruba            0.035
## 3    3 Afghanistan            0.035
```

1.6.2.3 Edges list

```
per_route <- france.trade %>%
  select(source, destination)

# (a) Join nodes id for source column
edges <- per_route %>%
  left_join(nodes, by = c("source" = "label")) %>%
  rename(from = id)

# (b) Join nodes id for destination column
edges <- edges %>%
  left_join(nodes, by = c("destination" = "label")) %>%
  rename(to = id)

# (c) Select/keep only the columns from and to
```

```
dges <- select(edges, from, to)
ead(edges, 3)

# # A tibble: 3 x 2
#    from     to
#   <int> <int>
# 1     1     2
# 2     1     3
# 3     1     4
```

.6.2.4 Create the treemap

3. Create network object and visualize:

- Network object:

```
rade.graph <- tbl_graph(
 nodes = nodes, edges = edges, directed = TRUE
 )
```

- Visualize. The ggpubr package is required to generate color palette:

```
 Generate colors for each country
equire(ggpubr)
ols <- get_palette("Dark2", nrow(france.trade)+1)

 Visualize
et.seed(123)
graph(trade.graph, 'treemap', weight = "trade.percentage") +
   geom_node_tile(aes(fill = label), size = 0.25, color = "white")+
 geom_node_text(
   aes(label = paste(label, trade.percentage, sep = "\n"),
      size = trade.percentage), color = "white"
   )+
 scale_fill_manual(values = cols)+
 scale_size(range = c(0, 6) )+
 theme_void()+
 theme(legend.position = "none")
```

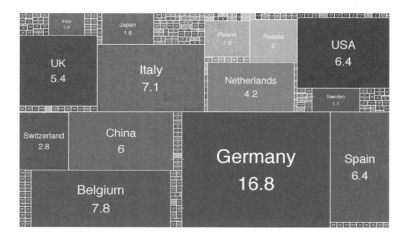

1.6.2.5 Create a choropleth map

- (1) Take the world map and Color each country according to the trading percentage with France.

- (2) Draw the map and color France in red

```
require("map")
# (1)
world_map <- map_data("world")
france.trade <- france.trade %>%
  left_join(world_map, by = c("destination" = "region"))
# (2)
ggplot(france.trade, aes(long, lat, group = group))+
  geom_polygon(aes(fill = trade.percentage ), color = "white")+
  geom_polygon(data = subset(world_map, region == "France"),
               fill = "red")+ # draw france in red
  scale_fill_gradientn(colours =c("lightgray", "yellow", "green"))+
  theme_void()
```

1.6.3 Dendrogram layout

Dendrogram layout are suited for hierarchical graph visualization, that is graph structures including trees and hierarchies.

In this section, we'll compute hierarchical clustering using the USArrests data set. The output is visualized as a dendrogram tree.

1. compute hierarchical clustering using the USArrests data set;
2. then convert the result into a tbl_graph.

```
res.hclust <- scale(USArrests) %>%
  dist() %>% hclust()
res.tree <- as.dendrogram(res.hclust)
```

3. Visualize the dendrogram tree. Key function: geom_edge_diagonal() and geom_edge_elbow()

```
# Diagonal layout
ggraph(res.tree, layout = "dendrogram") +
  geom_edge_diagonal() +
  geom_node_text(
    aes(label = label), angle = 90, hjust = 1,
    size = 3
    )+
  ylim(-1.5, NA)+
  theme_minimal()
```

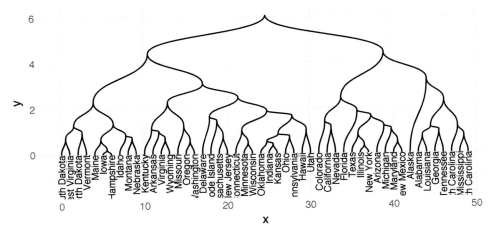

```
# Elbow layout
ggraph(res.tree, layout = "dendrogram") +
  geom_edge_elbow() +
  geom_node_text(
    aes(label = label), angle = 90, hjust = 1,
    size = 3
    )+
  ylim(-1.5, NA)+theme_minimal()
```

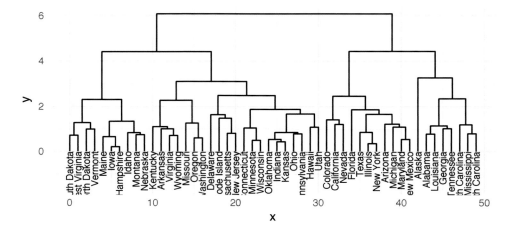

1.7   Read more

- Introduction to ggraph: Edges[1], Nodes[2] and layouts[3]
- Network Visualization with ggplot2[4]

---

[1]https://www.data-imaginist.com/2017/ggraph-introduction-edges/

[2]https://www.data-imaginist.com/2017/ggraph-introduction-nodes/

[3]https://www.data-imaginist.com/2017/ggraph-introduction-layouts/

[4]https://journal.r-project.org/archive/2017/RJ-2017-023/RJ-2017-023.pdf

Chapter 2

Network Analysis and Manipulation

This chapter describes how to manipulate and analyze a network graph in R using the `tidygraph` package.

The `tidygraph` package provides a tidy framework to easily manipulate different types of relational data, including: graph, network and trees.

In the tidygraph framework, network data are considered as two tidy data tables, one describing the node data and the other is for edge data. The package provides a simple solution to switch between the two tables and provides `dplyr` verbs for manipulating them.

You will learn methods for detecting important or central entities in a network graph. We'll also introduce how to detect community (or cluster) in a network.

2.1 Load required packages

- `tidyverse` for general data manipulation and visualization.
- `tidygraph` for manipulating and analyzing network graphs.
- `ggraph` for visualizing network objects created using the tidygraph package.

```
library(tidyverse)
library(tidygraph)
library(ggraph)
```

2.2 Create network objects

Key R functions:

- `tbl_graph()`. Creates a network object from nodes and edges data
- `as_tbl_graph()`. Converts network data and objects to a tbl_graph network.

Demo data set: `phone.call2` data [in the `navdata` R package], which is a list containing the nodes and the edges list prepared in the chapter 1.

15

2.2.1   Use tbl_graph

- Create a tbl_graph network object using the phone call data:

```
library("navdata")
data("phone.call2")
phone.net <- tbl_graph(
  nodes = phone.call2$nodes,
  edges = phone.call2$edges,
  directed = TRUE
  )
```

- Visualize:

```
ggraph(phone.net, layout = "graphopt") +
  geom_edge_link(width = 1, colour = "lightgray") +
  geom_node_point(size = 4, colour = "#00AFBB") +
  geom_node_text(aes(label = label), repel = TRUE)+
  theme_graph()
```

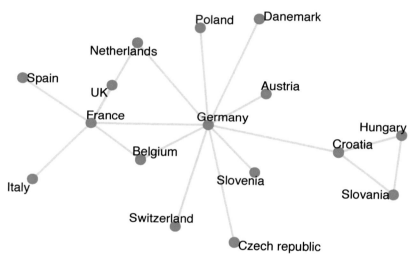

2.2.2   Use as_tbl_graph R function

One can also use the as_tbl_graph() function to converts the following data structure and network objects:

- data.frame, list and matrix data [R base]
- igraph network objects [igraph package]
- network network objects [network pakage]
- dendrogram and hclust [stats package]
- Node [data.tree package]
- phylo and evonet [ape package]
- graphNEL, graphAM, graphBAM [graph package (in Bioconductor)]

In the following example, we'll create a correlation matrix network graph. The `mtcars` data set will be used.

Compute the correlation matrix between cars using the `corrr` package:

- (1) Use the mtcars data set

- (2) Compute the correlation matrix: `correlate()`

- (3) Convert the upper triangle to NA: `shave()`

- (4) Stretch the correlation data frame into long format

- (5) Keep only high correlation

```
library(corrr)
res.cor <- mtcars [, c(1, 3:6)] %>%   # (1)
  t() %>% correlate() %>%             # (2)
  shave(upper = TRUE) %>%             # (3)
  stretch(na.rm = TRUE) %>%           # (4)
  filter(r >= 0.998)                  # (5)
res.cor

## # A tibble: 59 x 3
##                 x              y      r
##              <chr>          <chr>  <dbl>
## 1      Mazda RX4 Mazda RX4 Wag 1.000
## 2      Mazda RX4      Merc 230 1.000
## 3      Mazda RX4      Merc 280 0.999
## 4      Mazda RX4     Merc 280C 0.999
## 5      Mazda RX4    Merc 450SL 0.998
## 6 Mazda RX4 Wag      Merc 230 1.000
## # ... with 53 more rows
```

Create the correlation network graph:

```
set.seed(1)
cor.graph <- as_tbl_graph(res.cor, directed = FALSE)
ggraph(cor.graph) +
  geom_edge_link() +
  geom_node_point() +
  geom_node_text(
    aes(label = name), size = 3, repel = TRUE
    ) +
  theme_graph()
```

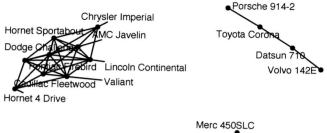

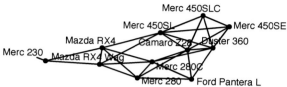

2.3   Print out a network object

```
cor.graph
```

```
## # A tbl_graph: 24 nodes and 59 edges
## #
## # An undirected simple graph with 3 components
## #
## # Node Data: 24 x 1 (active)
##                name
##               <chr>
## 1        Mazda RX4
## 2    Mazda RX4 Wag
## 3        Datsun 710
## 4    Hornet 4 Drive
## 5 Hornet Sportabout
## 6          Valiant
## # ... with 18 more rows
## #
## # Edge Data: 59 x 3
##    from    to    r
##   <int> <int> <dbl>
## 1     1     2 1.000
## 2     1    20 1.000
## 3     1     8 0.999
## # ... with 56 more rows
```

The output shows:

- a tbl_graph object with 24 nodes and 59 edges. Nodes are the car names and the edges are the correlation links.
- the first six rows of "Node Data"" and the first three of "Edge Data".
- that the Node Data is **active**.

The notion of an active tibble within a tbl_graph object makes it possible to manipulate the data in one tibble at a time. The nodes tibble is activated by default, but you can change which tibble is active with the `activate()` function.

If you want to rearrange the rows in the edges tibble to list those with the highest "r" first, you could use `activate()` and then `arrange()`. For example, type the following R code:

```
cor.graph %>%
  activate(edges) %>%
  arrange(desc(r))
```

> Note that, to extract the current active data as a tibble, you can use the function `as_tibble(cor.graph)`.

2.4 Network graph manipulation

With the `tidygraph` package, you can easily manipulate the nodes and the edges data in the network graph object using `dplyr` verbs. For example, you can add new columns or rename columns in the nodes/edges data.

You can also filter and arrange the data. Note that, applying `filter()`/`slice()` on node data will remove the edges terminating at the removed nodes.

In this section we'll manipulate the correlation network graph.

1. **Modify the nodes data**:

   - (a) Group the cars by the "cyl" variable (number of cylinders) in the original mtcars data set. We'll color the cars by groups.

   - (b) Join the group info to the nodes data

   - (c) Rename the column "name", in the nodes data, to "label"

You can use the `dplyr` verbs as follow:

```
# Car groups info
cars.group <- data_frame(
  name = rownames(mtcars),
  cyl = as.factor(mtcars$cyl)
)

# Modify the nodes data
cor.graph <- cor.graph %>%
  activate(nodes) %>%
  left_join(cars.group, by = "name") %>%
  rename(label = name)
```

2. **Modify the edge data**. Rename the column "r" to "weight".

```
cor.graph <- cor.graph %>%
  activate(edges) %>%
  rename(weight = r)
```

3. **Display the final modified graphs object**:

```
cor.graph
```

```
## # A tbl_graph: 24 nodes and 59 edges
## #
## # An undirected simple graph with 3 components
## #
## # Edge Data: 59 x 3 (active)
##     from     to weight
##    <int> <int>   <dbl>
## 1     1     2  1.000
## 2     1    20  1.000
## 3     1     8  0.999
## 4     1     9  0.999
## 5     1    11  0.998
## 6     2    20  1.000
## # ... with 53 more rows
## #
## # Node Data: 24 x 2
##             label     cyl
##             <chr> <fctr>
## 1       Mazda RX4       6
## 2 Mazda RX4 Wag       6
## 3      Datsun 710       4
## # ... with 21 more rows
```

4. **Visualize the correlation network**.

- Change the edges width according to the variable weight
- Scale the edges width by setting the minimum width to 0.2 and the maximum to 1.
- Change the color of cars (nodes) according to the grouping variable cyl.

```
set.seed(1)
ggraph(cor.graph) +
  geom_edge_link(aes(width = weight), alpha = 0.2) +
  scale_edge_width(range = c(0.2, 1)) +
  geom_node_point(aes(color = cyl), size = 2) +
  geom_node_text(aes(label = label), size = 3, repel = TRUE) +
  theme_graph()
```

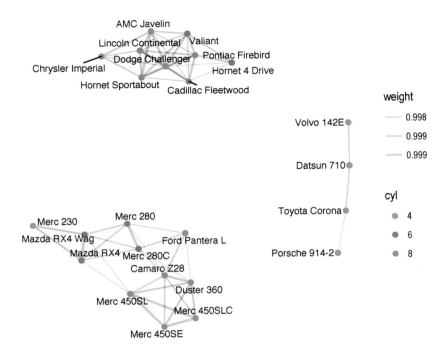

2.5 Network analysis

In this sections, we described methods for detecting important or central entities in a network graph. We'll also introduce how to detect community (or cluster) in a network.

2.5.1 Centrality

Centrality is an important concept when analyzing network graph. The centrality of a node / edge measures how central (or important) is a node or edge in the network.

We consider an entity important, if he has connections to many other entities. Centrality describes the number of edges that are connected to nodes.

There many types of scores that determine centrality. One of the famous ones is the pagerank algorithm that was powering Google Search in the beginning.

Examples of common approaches of measuring centrality include:

- **betweenness centrality**. The betweenness centrality for each nodes is the number of the shortest paths that pass through the nodes.

- **closeness centrality**. Closeness centrality measures how many steps is required to access every other nodes from a given nodes. It describes the distance of a node to all other nodes. The more central a node is, the closer it is to all other nodes.

- **eigenvector centrality**. A node is important if it is linked to by other important nodes. The centrality of each node is proportional to the sum of the centralities of those nodes to which it is connected. In general, nodes with high eigenvector centralities are those which are linked to many other nodes which are, in turn, connected to many others (and so on).

- **Hub** and **authority centarlities** are generalization of eigenvector centrality. A high hub node points to many good authorities and a high authority node receives from many good hubs.

The `tidygraph` package contains more than 10 centrality measures, prefixed with the term `centrality_`. These measures include:

```
centrality_authority()
```

```
centrality_betweenness()
```

```
centrality_closeness()
```

```
centrality_hub()
```

```
centrality_pagerank()
```

```
centrality_eigen()
```

```
centrality_edge_betweenness()
```

All of these centrality functions returns a numeric vector matching the nodes (or edges in the case of 'centrality_edge_betweenness()).

In the following examples, we'll use the phone call network graph. We'll change the color and the size of nodes according to their values of centrality.

```
set.seed(123)
phone.net %>%
  activate(nodes) %>%
  mutate(centrality = centrality_authority()) %>%
  ggraph(layout = "graphopt") +
  geom_edge_link(width = 1, colour = "lightgray") +
  geom_node_point(aes(size = centrality, colour = centrality)) +
  geom_node_text(aes(label = label), repel = TRUE)+
  scale_color_gradient(low = "yellow", high = "red")+
  theme_graph()
```

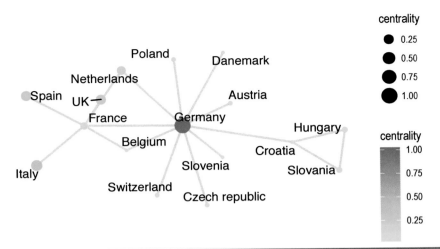

For a given problem at hand, you can test the different centrality score to decide which centrality measure makes most sense for your specific question.

2.5.2 Clustering

Clustering is a common operation in network analysis and it consists of grouping nodes based on the graph topology.

It's sometimes referred to as community detection based on its commonality in social network analysis.

Many clustering algorithms from are available in the `tidygraph` package and prefixed with the term `group_`. These include:

- **Infomap community finding**. It groups nodes by minimizing the expected description length of a random walker trajectory. R function: `group_infomap()`
- **Community structure detection based on edge betweenness**. It groups densely connected nodes. R function: `group_edge_betweenness()`.

In the following example, we'll use the correlation network graphs to detect clusters or communities:

```
set.seed(123)
cor.graph %>%
  activate(nodes) %>%
   mutate(community = as.factor(group_infomap())) %>%
  ggraph(layout = "graphopt") +
  geom_edge_link(width = 1, colour = "lightgray") +
  geom_node_point(aes(colour = community), size = 4) +
  geom_node_text(aes(label = label), repel = TRUE)+
  theme_graph()
```

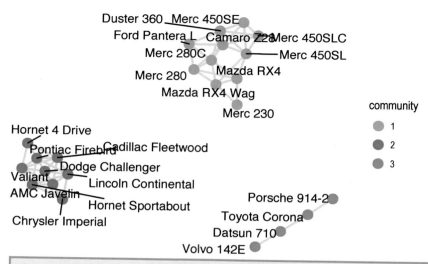

Three communities are detected.

2.6　Read more

- Thomas Lin Pedersen. Introducing tidygraph. https://www.data-imaginist.com/2017/introducing-tidygraph/
- Shirin Glander. Network analysis of Game of Thrones. https://datascienceplus.com/network-analysis-of-game-of-thrones/

Chapter 3

Interactive Network Visualization

This chapter describes two key R packages for creating interactive network graphs. These packages include:

- **visNetwork** (Almende B.V. et al., 2017). Creates an interactive network visualization using the **vis.js** javascript library (`http://visjs.org/`).
- **networkD3** (Allaire et al., 2017). Creates a D3 JavaScript Network Graphs from R.

You'll learn how to:

- Create a classic network graph that is interactive
- Make an interactive sankey diagram, useful for network flow visualization
- Visualize, interactively, classification and regression trees

3.1   Load demo data sets and R package

We'll use the `phone.call2` data [in the `navdata` R package], which is a list containing the nodes and the edges list prepared in the chapter 1 from the `phone.call` data.

Start by loading the tidyverse R package and the phone.call2 demo data sets:

```r
library(tidyverse)

library("navdata")
data("phone.call2")
nodes <- phone.call2$nodes
edges <- phone.call2$edges
```

3.2   networkD3 R package

3.2.1   Key features

Can be used to easily create an interactive sankey diagram, as well as, other network layout such as dendrogram, radial and diagnonal networks.

3.2.2   Key R functions and options

Key R functions:

forceNetwork(). Creates a D3 JavaScript force directed network graph

```
forceNetwork(Links, Nodes, Source, Target,
             Value, NodeID, Nodesize, Group)
```

Key Arguments:

- Links: edges list. **Edge IDs should start with 0**
- Nodes: Nodes list. **Node IDs should start with 0**
- Source, Target: the names of the column, in the edges data, containing the network source and target variables, respectively.
- Value: the name of the column, in the edge data, containing the weight values for edges. Used to indicate how wide the links are.
- NodeID: the name of the column, in the nodes data, containing the node IDs. Used for labeling the nodes.
- Nodesize: the name of the column, in the nodes data, with some value to vary the node radius's with.
- Group: the name of the column, in the nodes data, specifying the group of each node.

3.2.3   Prepare nodes and edes data

As specified above, the IDs in nodes and edges lists should be numeric values starting with 0. This can be easily done by substracting 1 from the existing IDs in the two data frames.

1. Prepare the nodes and the edges data:

```
nodes_d3 <- mutate(nodes, id = id - 1)
edges_d3 <- mutate(edges, from = from - 1, to = to - 1)
```

2. Create the interactive network:

```
library("networkD3")
forceNetwork(
  Links = edges_d3, Nodes = nodes_d3,
  Source = "from", Target = "to",      # so the network is directed.
  NodeID = "label", Group = "id", Value = "weight",
  opacity = 1, fontSize = 16, zoom = TRUE
  )
```

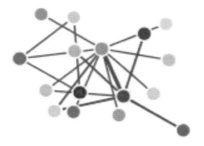

Figure 3.1: Interactive network using networkD3

> Note that, a color is attributed to each group. Here, as we specified the column "id" as the node Group value, we have different colors for each individual nodes.

3.2.4 Create sankey diagram

You can create a d3-styled sankey diagram[1]. A Sankey diagram is a good fit for the phone call data. There are not too many nodes in the data, making it easier to visualize the flow of phone calls.

Create a sankey diagram:

```
sankeyNetwork(
  Links = edges_d3, Nodes = nodes_d3,
  Source = "from", Target = "to",
  NodeID = "label", Value = "weight",
  fontSize = 16, unit = "Letter(s)")
```

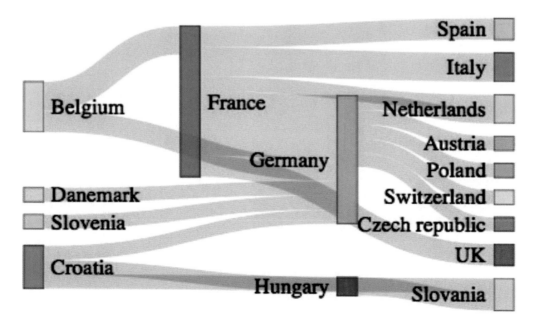

Figure 3.2: Sankey Diagram

---

[1]https://bost.ocks.org/mike/sankey/

Other hierarchical layouts exist in the network3D package to visualize tree-like graphs. In the example below, we start by computing hierarchical clustering using a sample of the USArrests data set:

```
set.seed(123)
hc <- USArrests %>% sample_n(15) %>%
  scale() %>% dist() %>%
  hclust(method = "complete")
```

3.2.5   Other network layouts

- **dendroNetwork**:

```
dendroNetwork(hc, fontSize = 15)
```

Figure 3.3: Dendro network

Other alternatives are:

- **radialNetwork**:

```
radialNetwork(
  as.radialNetwork(hc), fontSize = 15
  )
```

- **diagonalNetwork**:

```
diagonalNetwork(
  as.radialNetwork(hc), fontSize = 15
  )
```

3.3 visNetwork R package

3.3.1 Key features

- Creates interactive network graphs.
- Possible to customize nodes and edge as you want.
- Can be used to directly visualize interactively a network generated with the `igraph` package.
- Can be used to visualize recursive partitioning and regression trees generated with the `rpart` package.
- Possible to use images and icons for node shapes.
- Supports `igraph` layouts

3.3.2 Key R function and options

Key R function:

```
visNetwork(
  nodes = NULL, edges = NULL,
  width = NULL, height = NULL,
  main = NULL, submain = NULL, footer = NULL
  )
```

Key Arguments:

- `nodes`: nodes list information. Should contain at least the column "id". See `visNodes()` for more options to control nodes. Other colums can be included in the data, such as:
  - "id" : id of the node, needed in edges information
  - "label" : label of the node
  - "group" : group of the node. Groups can be configure with `visGroups()`.
  - "value" : size of the node
  - "title" : tooltip of the node
  - ...
- `edges`: edges list information. Required at least columns "from" and "to". See `visEdges()` for more options to control edges.
  - "from" : node id of begin of the edge
  - "to" : node id of end of the edge
  - "label" : label of the edge
  - "value" : size of the node
  - "title" : tooltip of the node
  - ...

3.3.3 Create a classic network graphs

Note that, the function plots the labels for the nodes, using the "label" column in the node list.

You can move the nodes and the graph will use an algorithm to keep the nodes properly spaced. You can also zoom in and out on the plot and move it around to re-center it.

To have always the same network, you can use the function `visLayout(randomSeed = 12)`:

```
library("visNetwork")
visNetwork(nodes, edges) %>%
  visLayout(randomSeed = 12)
```

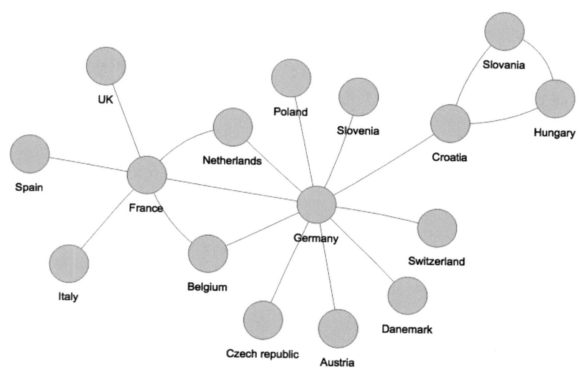

Figure 3.4: Classic network using visNetwork

Note that,

- `visNetwork` can use `igraph` layouts, which include a large variety of possible layouts.
- you can use `visIgraph()` to directly visualize an `igraph` network object.

If you want to control the width of edges according to a variable, you should include the column "width" in the edge list data. You should manually calculate and scale the edge width.

In the following R code, we'll customize the `visNetwork()` output by using an `igraph` layout and changing the edges width.

First add the column width in the edges list data frame. Set the minimum width to 1:

```
edges <- mutate(edges, width = 1 + weight/5)
```

Create the network graph with the variable edge widths and the igraph layout = "layout_with_fr".

```
visNetwork(nodes, edges) %>%
  visIgraphLayout(layout = "layout_with_fr") %>%
  visEdges(arrows = "middle") %>%
  visLayout(randomSeed = 12)
```

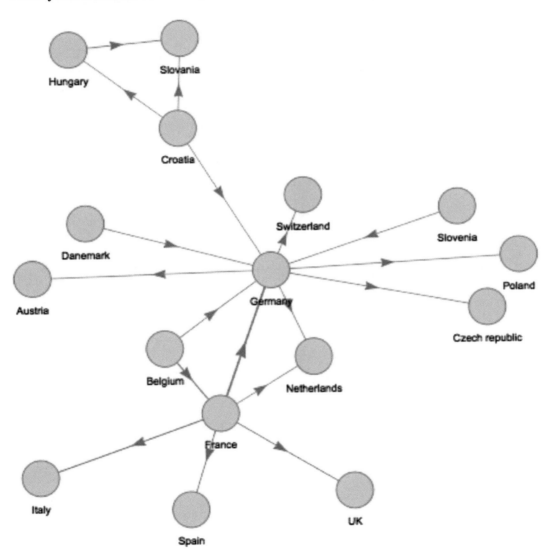

Figure 3.5: Network with igraph layout and arrows

3.3.4 Visualize classification and regression trees

As mentioned above, you can visualize classification and regression trees generated using the **rpart** package.

Key function: `visTree()` [in `visNetwork version >= 2.0.0`].

For example, to visualize a classification tree, type the following R code:

```
# Compute
library(rpart)
res <- rpart(Species~., data=iris)

# Visualize
visTree(res, main = "Iris classification Tree",
        width = "80%",  height = "400px")
```

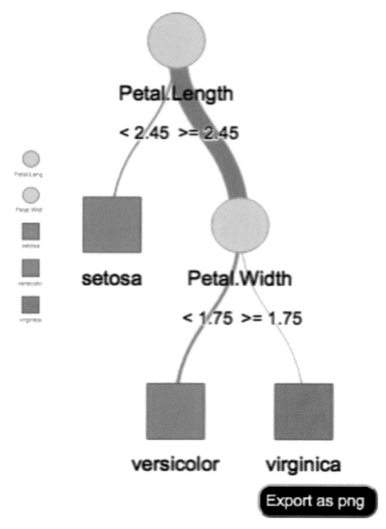

Figure 3.6: Classificcation tree

Bibliography

Allaire, J., Gandrud, C., Russell, K., and Yetman, C. (2017). *networkD3: D3 JavaScript Network Graphs from R.* R package version 0.4.

Almende B.V., Thieurmel, B., and Robert, T. (2017). *visNetwork: Network Visualization using 'vis.js' Library.* R package version 2.0.1.

file., S. A. (2017). *igraph: Network Analysis and Visualization.* R package version 1.1.2.

Pedersen, T. L. (2017a). *ggraph: An Implementation of Grammar of Graphics for Graphs and Networks.* R package version 1.0.0.

Pedersen, T. L. (2017b). *tidygraph: A Tidy API for Graph Manipulation.* R package version 1.0.0.

Tyner, S., Briatte, F., and Hofmann, H. (2017). Network Visualization with ggplot2. *The R Journal*, 9(1):27–59.

Made in the USA
Middletown, DE
27 July 2021